On the Move

by Barbara Wood

PEARSON
Scott Foresman

Editorial Offices: Glenview, Illinois • Parsippany, New Jersey • New York, New York
Sales Offices: Needham, Massachusetts • Duluth, Georgia • Glenview, Illinois
Coppell, Texas • Sacramento, California • Mesa, Arizona

Jo is going to see a friend.
Jo will ride a bus.

Andy is going to see a friend.
Andy will go by airplane.

Long ago, people had to walk.

People learned that a donkey could help.

People made rafts.
They also built ships.

Ford Model T Car

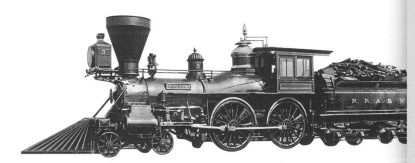

Steam Engine Train

There was a new **invention**.
This invention was an **engine**.
Cars and trains have engines.

New cars are fast.
New trains are fast too.

The story of travel is not over.
How will travel change?

Glossary

engine a machine that makes things move

invention something new